Sports Illustrated KIDS

FANTASY FOOTBALL MATH

USING STATS TO SCORE BIG
IN YOUR LEAGUE

BY MATT DOEDEN

CAPSTONE PRESS
a capstone imprint

Sports Illustrated Kids Fantasy Sports Math is published by Capstone Press,
1710 Roe Crest Drive, North Mankato, Minnesota 56003.
www.mycapstone.com

Library of Congress Cataloging-in-Publication Data
Names: Doeden, Matt.
Title: Fantasy football math : using stats to score big in your league / by Matt Doeden.
Description: Mankato, Minnesota : Capstone Press, [2017] | Series: Sports Illustrated Kids.
  Fantasy Sports Math | Includes bibliographical references and index. | Audience: Ages: 8-12. |
  Audience: Grades: 4 to 6. | Description based on print version record and CIP data provided by
  publisher; resource not viewed.
Identifiers: LCCN 2015051401 (print) | LCCN 2015049425 (ebook) | ISBN 9781515721758 (eBook PDF) |
  ISBN 9781515721680 (library binding) | ISBN 9781515721710 (paperback)
Subjects: LCSH: Fantasy football (Game)—Mathematical models—Juvenile literature.
Classification: LCC GV1202.F34 (print) | LCC GV1202.F34 D64 2017 (ebook) |
  DDC 793.93001/5118—dc23
LC record available at http://lccn.loc.gov/2015051401

Summary: Describes how to use statistics and math to create and run a successful fantasy football team.

Editorial Credits
Aaron Sautter, editor; Sarah Bennett, designer; Eric Gohl, media researcher; Katy LaVigne, production specialist

Photo Credits
Newscom: Cal Sport Media/Tim Warner, 4-5, Icon SMI/Bob Levey, 11, Icon SMI/Cliff Welch, 10, 22, Icon
Sportswire/Chris Williams, 28–29, Icon Sportswire/Kellen Micah, 12, UPI/Bill Greenblatt, 18-19, ZUMA Press/
Loren Elliott, 26; Shutterstock: Alesandro14, 2-3; Sports Illustrated: Al Tielemans, cover, 13, 20-21, 23, Damian
Strohmeyer, 27, David E. Klutho, 24-25, John W. McDonough, 8-9, Robert Beck, 16-17, Simon Bruty, 6-7, 14-15

Design Elements: Shutterstock

TABLE OF CONTENTS

PREPARE TO DOMINATE

First you build an all-star team of your favorite National Football League (NFL) players. You cheer when one player streaks into the end zone. Or you groan when another player coughs up the ball. You bite your nails, hoping your running back can bust out with a winning score. Then you celebrate when your team comes out on top. Welcome to the wild world of fantasy football!

You don't need to be built like a linebacker to win at this game. Some knowledge of pro football and its players is a good start. But knowing how football is played isn't enough. Fantasy sports are all about **statistics**. And stats are all about math. To dominate your league, you'll have to master the numbers. In fantasy football, knowing the math is almost as important as knowing the game of football itself.

---

statistics—numbers, facts, or other data collected about a specific subject

CHAPTER 1

LIGHTING UP THE SCOREBOARD

In the NFL, the best teams score a lot of points. Fantasy football is the same way. Think quick—Atlanta Falcons quarterback Matt Ryan just rifled a 60-yard touchdown pass to receiver Julio Jones. That's good news for you. They're both on your fantasy team. How many points did you just score?

Offensive Scoring: The Basics

Hold on. We can't answer that question just yet. There's no single way to score points in fantasy football. Fantasy leagues use a wide range of scoring systems. Check out this chart for a few basic scoring models.

	TD HEAVY SYSTEM	BALANCED SYSTEM	YARDAGE HEAVY SYSTEM
Passing TD	6 points	4 points	4 points
Rushing/Receiving TD	6 points	6 points	6 points
Passing Yardage	1 point per 150 yards	1 point per 50 yards	1 point per 25 yards
Rushing/Receiving Yardage	1 point per 50 yards	1 point per 20 yards	1 point per 10 yards
Fumbles/Interceptions	-2 points	-2 points	-2 points

Now we can do the math for that big play earlier. Using a balanced scoring system, figure out the players' points.

Matt Ryan: 4 points (TD pass) + 1 point (Yardage) = 5 points

Julio Jones: 6 points (TD catch) + 3 points (Yardage) = 9 points

Ryan and Jones just scored a combined 14 points for your team. Now see if you can do the math using the other two systems. Find the answers at the bottom of the next page.

Julio Jones ⇒

Getting Defensive

Quarterbacks, running backs, and wide receivers get most of the fantasy football glory. Defenses and **special teams** often get overlooked. But a good defense can make all the difference for your team.

J. J. Watt ⇑

Most leagues feature scoring from both team defenses and special teams. So if you want a defensive star like the Houston Texans' J. J. Watt, you'll have to draft the entire D. Here's how basic defensive scoring works for many leagues.

Interception or Fumble Recovery	2 points
Safety	2 points
Blocked kick or punt	2 points
Sack	1 point
Defense/Special Team Touchdown	6 points

Let's say Houston's defense sacks Indianapolis Colts quarterback Andrew Luck and forces a fumble. Watt scoops up the ball and dashes in for a touchdown. How many points did your team just score? Check to see if you got the right answer below.

FANTASY FACT

Many leagues also factor in points allowed by a team defense. For example, if your D earns a **shutout**, you may score 10 bonus points. But be careful. A bad defense could cost you points if it gives up a big score to the opposing team.

special teams—units used to handle kickoffs, punts, and field goal attempts

shutout—a game in which a defense holds the opposing team to zero points

Answer: 1 (Sack) + 2 (Fumble Recovery) + 6 (Defensive Touchdown) = 9 points

Don't Forget the Kicker

Kickers are often the forgotten players on a fantasy team. However, a solid kicker can often be your team's highest-scoring player for a week.

Basic scoring systems typically award kickers 3 points for a field goal and 1 point for an extra point. Many leagues also offer bonus points for longer field goals. A kick of 40 or more yards may be worth 4 points. A boot of 50 yards or more may be worth 5 points. Meanwhile, some leagues also subtract 1 point for each missed kick.

Imagine your league uses a scoring system like this for kickers. You're watching your kicker line up for a 53-yard attempt. How many points are on the line? Check your answer below to see if you're right.

FANTASY POINT *EXPLOSION*
(BALANCED SCORING)

Rob Bironas, K, Tennessee Titans

2007 Season, Week 7

8 Field Goals; 2 Extra Points

Balanced League Fantasy Points: 26

Answer: 5 points for a successful kick, but -1 point if he misses. That's a 6-point swing.

Rob Bironas ⇒

LeSean McCoy

PPR Leagues

PPR leagues offer a fun scoring twist. PPR stands for "point per **reception**." In PPR leagues each catch a player makes is worth a bonus point. Imagine your team is tied with your opponent's team. It's the final seconds of the last game of the week. Your players are done, but your opponent still has Buffalo Bills running back LeSean McCoy on the field. He catches a quick pass, but the defense buries him for a 5-yard loss. Awesome—that seals the win for you, right? Not so fast. In a PPR league McCoy just scored a point, even though he lost a few yards. You just lost your fantasy game.

Fractional Scoring

Now try this. Say you have Kansas City Chiefs running back Jamaal Charles, and he has 80 yards on the day. You need just one more point from him to win your game. Charles gets the ball and gashes the defense for a 19-yard gain. Unfortunately that big run doesn't do you any good. In a balanced scoring system both 80 yards and 99 yards are worth 4 points. But with **fractional scoring**, leagues ignore round numbers. In a balanced fractional league, each yard might be worth 0.05 points. Now using this scoring system, how many points did Charles earn on his 99 yards? Check your answer at the bottom of the page.

Jamaal Charles

FANTASY FACT

Some leagues even use individual defensive players (IDP) instead of full team defenses. These players earn points for making tackles, defending passes, and sacking the opposing quarterback.

reception—a pass caught by a player

fractional scoring—a scoring system that awards a fraction of a point for each yard gained

Answer: 99 × 0.05 = 4.95 points

CHAPTER 2

BUILDING A CHAMPION

Draft day. These two words give fantasy fans the chills. It's the most important day of the season. Fantasy players dream of glory as they try to draft the league's best team. Time to build a champion!

The Snake Draft

The most common type of fantasy draft is the snake draft. The snake is done in **rounds**. Team owners take turns picking players until their rosters are full. The draft order flips each round. So if you have the first pick in Round 1, you won't pick again until the end of Round 2. But if you get the last pick in Round 1, you get to pick again right away at the start of Round 2.

Say there are 13 top players you'd like for your team. In a 10-team league, which picks would help you get two of them? Pick number one guarantees that you can grab the best possible player. But the rest will probably be gone before you pick again. However, if you pick at number 8, you can pick again at number 13 in round 2. So you'll want either pick 8, 9, or 10 to get two of your top 13 choices.

ROUND	TEAM 1	TEAM 2	TEAM 3	TEAM 4	TEAM 5	TEAM 6	TEAM 7	TEAM 8	TEAM 9	TEAM 10
1	Pick 1	Pick 2	Pick 3	Pick 4	Pick 5	Pick 6	Pick 7	Pick 8	Pick 9	Pick 10
2	Pick 20	Pick 19	Pick 18	Pick 17	Pick 16	Pick 15	Pick 14	Pick 13	Pick 12	Pick 11

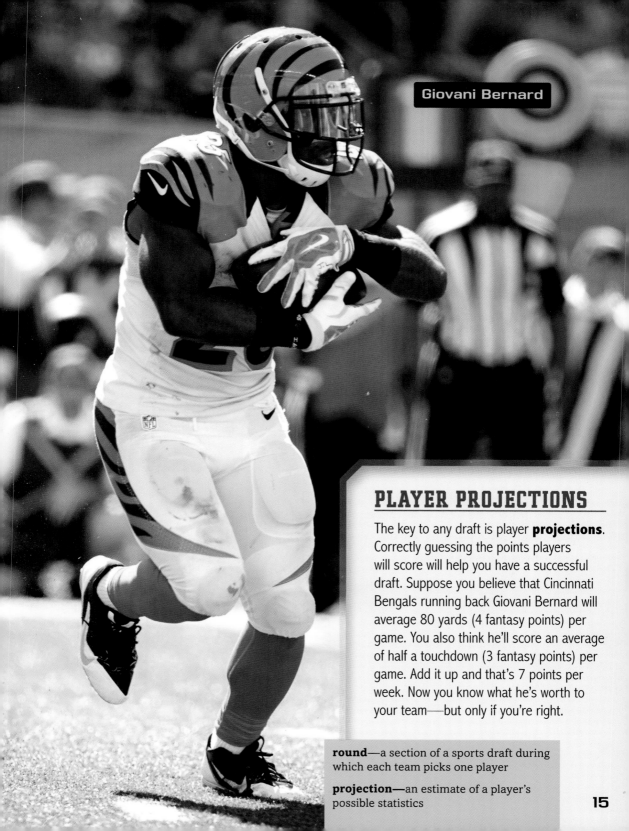

Giovani Bernard

PLAYER PROJECTIONS

The key to any draft is player **projections**. Correctly guessing the points players will score will help you have a successful draft. Suppose you believe that Cincinnati Bengals running back Giovani Bernard will average 80 yards (4 fantasy points) per game. You also think he'll score an average of half a touchdown (3 fantasy points) per game. Add it up and that's 7 points per week. Now you know what he's worth to your team—but only if you're right.

round—a section of a sports draft during which each team picks one player

projection—an estimate of a player's possible statistics

15

Auction Time

If you like to spend money, then an auction draft might be for you. In these drafts each owner gets a fixed amount to spend, say $200. It's not real money. But you get to spend it like it is. Owners take turns opening the bidding on players. The highest bidder gets the player. The auction continues in this way until all the rosters are full.

You don't have to be a banker to nail an auction draft. But you do need to follow a **budget**. You need to think about where you'll get the most bang for your buck. Using **tiers** can help here. Tiers are groups of players with similar projections. Knowing where tiers start and end can help you find bargains. Take a look at these running back projections:

Clinton Portis ⇑

TIER	PLAYER	PROJECTED POINTS PER GAME
1	Adrian Peterson, Minnesota Vikings	12 points
1	Le'Veon Bell, Pittsburgh Steelers	11.5 points
1	Jamaal Charles, Kansas City Chiefs	11 points
2	Doug Martin, Tampa Bay Buccaneers	8.5 points
3	Todd Gurley, Los Angeles Rams	6 points
3	Devonta Freeman, Atlanta Falcons	5 points

budget—a plan for how to spend a fixed amount of money effectively

tier—a group of players at one position who are expected to score similar point totals

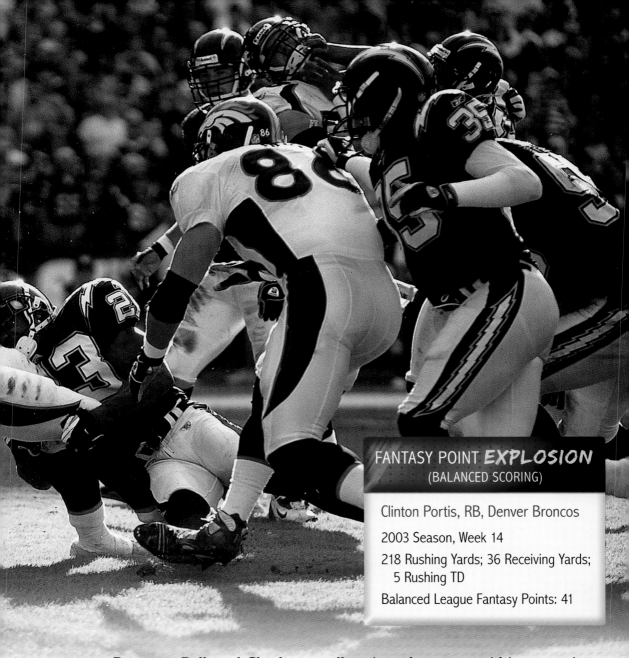

FANTASY POINT _EXPLOSION_
(BALANCED SCORING)

Clinton Portis, RB, Denver Broncos

2003 Season, Week 14

218 Rushing Yards; 36 Receiving Yards;
  5 Rushing TD

Balanced League Fantasy Points: 41

Peterson, Bell, and Charles are all projected to score within one point of each other. They're all in Tier 1. Say that Peterson and Bell each go for $60 in your league's auction. You should expect Charles to go for about the same. If you can get him for $50, that's a steal. But if those three are gone, you'll want to grab Martin fast. He's in Tier 2 all by himself! But be careful with your cash. Spending a lot on one player could leave you with little money left to fill out your roster.

Todd Gurley ⇒

Dynasty!

Dynasty leagues offer another twist to building a fantasy team. In dynasty leagues you get to keep some or all of your players from the previous season. This setup allows you to protect and build your team's core group of players from year to year. In a simple dynasty league, each owner gets to keep a few players, usually two or three, for the next season.

But picking your keepers can be tough. You have to consider each player's age, salary, and position. Imagine you've already kept Carolina Panthers quarterback Cam Newton and Los Angeles Rams running back Todd Gurley for your team. You need to decide on your third and final keeper. Which of the following players would be the best choice?

PLAYER	POSITION	AGE	SALARY	PROJECTED POINTS
Player 1	RB	26	$22	8 points per game
Player 2	WR	30	$15	7 points per game
Player 3	WR	22	$3	5 points per game

What do you do? You have to crunch all the numbers and make a decision. Player 1 looks like the surest thing. He puts up a lot of points, but he's also the most expensive. Plus you've kept one top-notch running back already. Player 2 provides good value for your money. But at age 30 he might be in decline. Player 3 is the least productive. But he's cheap and he's young. He may have several productive years ahead of him. He could be a bargain ... or a bust.

FANTASY POINT *IMPLOSION*
(BALANCED SCORING)

Peyton Manning, QB, Denver Broncos

2015 Season, Week 10

35 Passing Yards, 0 Passing TD, 4 Interceptions

Balanced League Fantasy Points: -8

CHAPTER 3

MANAGING YOUR TEAM

You've drafted a killer team. Now you can sit back and watch your team rack up the wins. Right? Wrong. It takes more than drafting skills to dominate your league. You need to also be a good manager.

Setting the Lineup

Each week you need to decide who will be your starters. You probably have a few players you'll want to start every week. But others will be week-to-week decisions. You'll have to base your choices on the players' stats, who's hot, who's healthy, and the defense each player is facing. Let's say that for one week you need to choose between two tight ends.

PLAYER	AVG. POINTS PER WEEK	DEFENSE FACED	AVG. TE POINTS ALLOWED
Greg Olsen, Carolina Panthers	9	New York Jets	3
Kyle Rudolph, Minnesota Vikings	5	Miami Dolphins	9

Olsen has been the better player. But the Jets have been tough on tight ends all year. Rudolph hasn't been as good overall. But tight ends have been scoring on the Dolphins. What do you do? Some owners prefer to start the better player no matter what. Others average the two scores to get a projection. For Olsen, you'd add his average to the Jets' average allowed: 9 + 3 = 12. Then divide that by two to get his projected points for that week: 6 points.

Now try the same for Rudolph. Check your answer on the next page. Which would be the better player to start?

Doug Martin

FANTASY POINT *EXPLOSION*
(BALANCED SCORING)

Doug Martin, RB,
Tampa Bay Buccaneers

2012 Season, Week 9

251 Rushing Yards, 4 Rushing TD,
   21 Receiving Yards

Balanced League Fantasy Points: 34

Transaction Time

You feel you drafted a great team. But team-building doesn't end there. To stay on top, you'll likely need to make roster moves, or **transactions**, throughout the season.

Suppose your quarterback is the Seattle Seahawks' Russell Wilson. In Week 7 Wilson gets injured and will be out for six weeks. Unfortunately, your backup is on a **bye week**, and you don't have any free roster spots. What do you do? Do you drop Wilson? It depends on how badly you need to win. If you're fighting to make the playoffs, you might have no choice. Say Wilson averages 14 points per game. But your backup, Kansas City Chiefs quarterback Alex Smith, averages only 9 points. The best available passer averages just 7 points per game.

Do you drop Wilson or Smith and add the new player? An extra 7 points could be the difference between winning and losing that week. But if you drop either of your players, someone else could grab him. You'd like to keep Wilson for the playoffs. However, hanging on to him is pointless if you don't make the playoffs. There's no easy answer here. It's all based on your team's situation.

Russell Wilson

transaction—a change on a team's roster, such as adding or dropping a player

bye week—a week in which certain NFL teams do not play a game

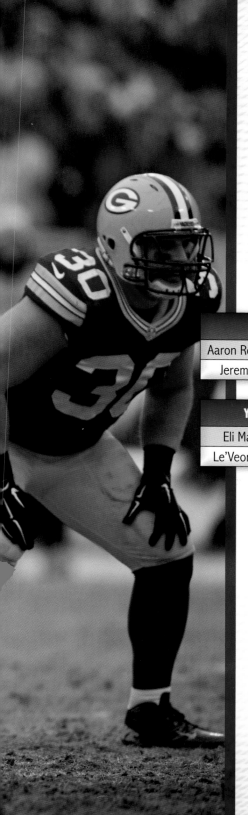

The Trading Block

There are two kinds of fantasy football owners. Some love their players like family. Others treat the league like a giant swap meet. Which are you?

It's easy to get attached to your guys. After all, you drafted them for a reason. But nothing can turn your season around like a blockbuster trade. When do you pull the trigger? Suppose someone makes you the following offer:

YOU GIVE UP	POSITION	AVG FANTASY POINTS/GAME
Aaron Rodgers, Green Bay Packers	QB	15
Jeremy Hill, Cincinnati Bengals	RB	8

YOU GET IN RETURN		
Eli Manning, New York Giants	QB	12
Le'Veon Bell, Pittsburgh Steelers	QB	14

You might love Aaron Rodgers and want to keep him. But you'll have to look long and hard at this offer. Which pair of players gives you the most combined points? Of course, you also have to consider factors such as player health and future opponents. Dynasty league owners will also have to think about their team's future. Rodgers could be a star quarterback for years to come. But based on the numbers alone, this is a trade that could put your team over the top. Making smart trades like this may help your team find championship glory.

Sweating Monday Night

Let's say your team is behind going into the Monday night game. But hope is not lost. All of your opponent's players are finished for the week. However, you have two spots left. One is for Dallas Cowboys quarterback Tony Romo. He averages 13 points per game.

The other open spot is for a wide receiver. But you have one from each NFL team playing on Monday night. You could go with Dallas' Dez Bryant. Or you could use Mike Evans from the Tampa Bay Buccaneers.

PLAYER	TEAM	AVG. POINTS PER GAME
Dez Bryant	Dallas	9 points
Mike Evans	Tampa Bay	9.5 points

Which one do you start? It might depend on how far you're behind. If you're down 15 or 20 points, Evans might be the choice. Why? You know that if Romo struggles, Bryant will likely have poor numbers as well. By using Evans, you're spreading out your chances for points across two teams.

Mike Evans

But what if you're down 30 points or more? If Romo puts up a pile of points, you know there's a good chance Bryant will too. That's because Romo and Bryant form a **tandem**. Quarterbacks and their star receivers often have big games together. Adding their fantasy points together could give you the win. So gambling on the tandem might be your best shot.

⇐ Dez Bryant

tandem—two players on a team who tend to score together, such as a quarterback and a wide receiver

27

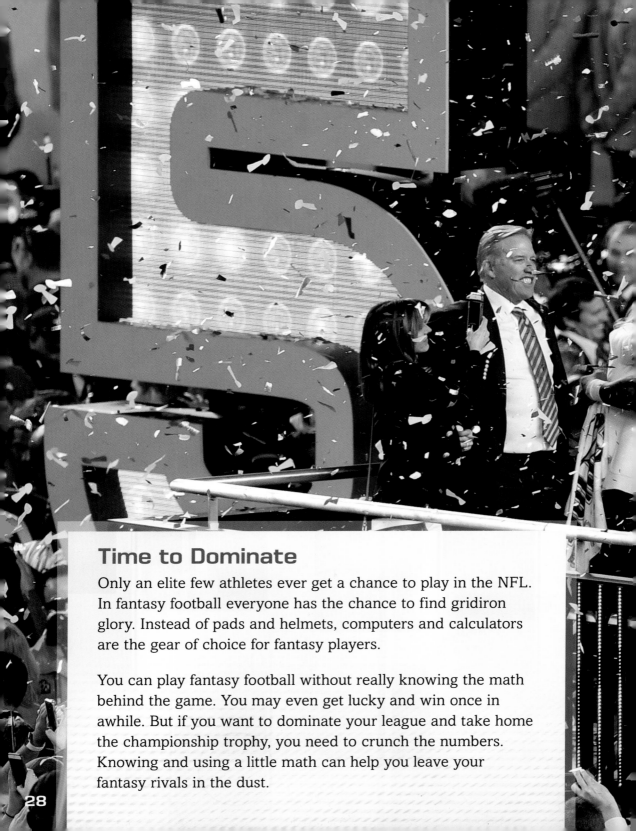

Time to Dominate

Only an elite few athletes ever get a chance to play in the NFL. In fantasy football everyone has the chance to find gridiron glory. Instead of pads and helmets, computers and calculators are the gear of choice for fantasy players.

You can play fantasy football without really knowing the math behind the game. You may even get lucky and win once in awhile. But if you want to dominate your league and take home the championship trophy, you need to crunch the numbers. Knowing and using a little math can help you leave your fantasy rivals in the dust.

Peyton Manning ⇓

FANTASY POINT *EXPLOSION*
(BALANCED SCORING)

Peyton Manning, QB,
Denver Broncos

2013 Season, Week 1
462 Passing Yards; 7 Passing TD
Balanced League Fantasy Points: 37

GLOSSARY

budget (BUH-juht)—a plan for how to spend a fixed amount of money effectively

bye week (BY WEEK)—a week in which certain NFL teams do not play a game

fractional scoring (FRAK-shuhn-uhl SKOR-ing)—a scoring system that awards a fraction of a point for each yard gained

projection (proh-JEK-shuhn)—an estimate of a player's possible statistics

reception (ri-SEP-shuhn)—a pass caught by a player

round (ROUND)—a section of a sports draft during which each team picks one player

shutout (SHUHT-out)—a game in which a defense holds the opposing team to zero points

special teams (SPESH-uhl TEEMS)—units used to handle kickoffs, punts, and field goal attempts

statistics (stuh-TISS-tiks)—numbers, facts, or other data collected about a specific subject

tandem (TAN-dum)—two players on a team who tend to score together, such as a quarterback and a wide receiver

tier (TEER)—a group of players at one position who are expected to score similar point totals

transaction (tran-ZAK-shuhn)—a change on a team's roster, such as adding or dropping a player, or making a trade

READ MORE

Frederick, Shane. *Football: The Math of the Game.* Sports Math. North Mankato, Minn.: Capstone Press, 2012.

Kortemeier, Todd. *Pro Football by the Numbers.* Pro Sports by the Numbers. North Mankato, Minn.: Capstone Press, 2016.

Loh-Hagan, Virginia. *Fantasy Football League.* D.I.Y. Make It Happen. Ann Arbor, Mich.: Cherry Lake Publishing, 2016.

INTERNET SITES

FactHound offers a safe, fun way to find Internet sites related to this book. All of the sites on FactHound have been researched by our staff.

Here's all you do:

Visit *www.facthound.com*

Type in this code: 9781515721680

Check out projects, games and lots more at
www.capstonekids.com

INDEX